MAGICAL YEARS TO LEARN WITH LIAM

Author Carolyn Ferrell Watts

Published by Larry Dean Watts Publishing

All Rights Reserved
Copyright © 2013 by Carolyn Ferrell Watts

This book is dedicated to Liam.

Contents

One - Introduction   5

Two - Born to Communicate
The infant survival system initiates bonding via body language. Reading body language remains a strong human ability for life.   **6**

Three - The Job of Parents
Assuring human growth to full potential requires providing a child's (a) basic physical needs (*nutrition, hygiene, sleep, etc.*), (b) safety, (c) love/belonging, (d) self-esteem, and (e) self-actualization.   **12**

Four - Magical Power of Choice
Making choices is a major role of humans that must be learned early. It helps to build esteem (*confidence, achievement, respect*) and self-actualization (*value, problem-solving, and creativity*).   **24**

Acknowledgments

The pictures shared by my grandchildren and their families, Krissy and Stephen, Frankie and Joe, Katie and Nick, and Olivia, inspired this book. Cheryl Ware, Ph.D., and Linda Fleming provided invaluable editing and encouragement. Daily discussions with my husband, Larry Watts, and his belief in me make the challenges of writing fun!

Introduction

Magical years to empower children: During the years from one to eight, robust neurological growth and desire to please caregivers enhance learning. Life events influence neural pathways, forming behavior patterns and coping skills for future years.

Parenting with an awareness of this can empower a child for success. It can also provide a climate conducive to a stable, enjoyable family relationship.

Communication, the initial focus of this book, enables connection with primary caregivers. This bond is vital for infant survival.

Emphasis on the job of parents reminds readers of crucial areas requiring attention when providing for and preparing infants, toddlers and children for life.

The final focal point on choices is a guide in teaching the process and wisdom of thinking about and choosing actions. The ability to make good choices is a basic role of humans that needs to be developed early.

Interactive Feature: Each "picture page" ends with a question designed to prompt a child's interaction and interest. May you and your child enjoy this book and find it to be very useful.

BORN TO COMMUNICATE

HELLO!
MY NAME IS LIAM.
WHAT IS YOUR NAME?
I CAN TALK WITH MY FACE.

This is my HAPPY FACE. It says,
"I AM HAPPY YOU ARE READING MY BOOK!"

😊   **Please show your HAPPY FACE.**

My CRYING FACE says,
"MY WORLD FEELS UNSAFE SO I FEEL SAD AND SCARED."

😊 **Please show your CRYING FACE.**

My LISTENING FACE says,

"I CAN HEAR YOU; I AM LEARNING TO TALK LIKE YOU."

😊 **Please show your LISTENING FACE.**

My THINKING FACE says,

"I AM THINKING ABOUT IT."

😊 **Please show your THINKING FACE.**

My SAD FACE says,
"PLEASE HELP ME STOP FEELING LIKE THIS!"

😊 **Please show your SAD FACE.**

My SLEEPY FACE says,
"*I WILL FEEL BETTER AFTER I REST*"

😊 **Please show your SLEEPY FACE.**

THE JOB OF PARENTS

WHAT ARE MOMMIES AND DADDIES FOR?

I think their job is to:
1) take care of us,
2) keep us safe,
3) love us, and
4) teach us how to make good choices.

- 😊 **Please tell what you think a mommy is for.**

- 😊 **Please tell what you think a daddy is for.**

MOMMY AND DADDY TAKE CARE OF ME.

They feed me healthy foods.

My cousin, Bodhi, and I like fruits and vegetables.

😊 **Please tell what you like to eat.**

MOMMY AND DADDY TEACH ME TO BE CLEAN.

I know my bath time is the same, every day.
The water is warm, not too hot or cold.
I like to wear goggles to keep my eyes dry.

 **Please tell what you play with in the bath.**

THEY SEE THAT I GET THE SLEEP I NEED.

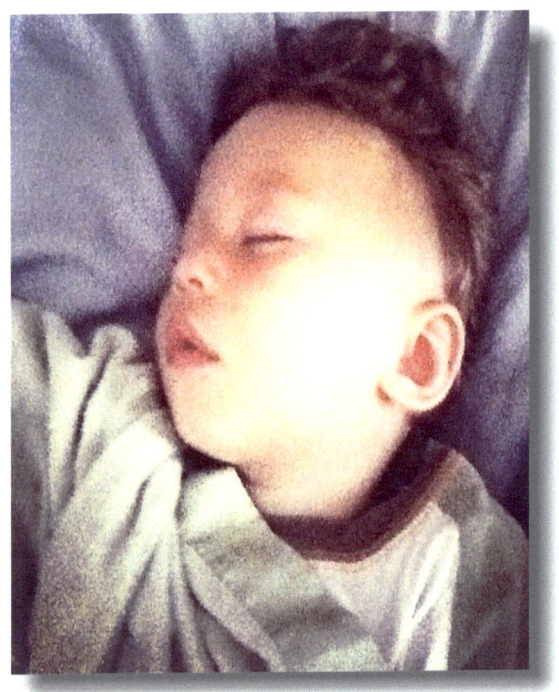

 **Please tell what you like to do before you sleep.**

MOMMY AND DADDY HELP ME FEEL SAFE.

I feel safe at Grandpa's farm.

I also feel safe at the beach!

I FEEL SAFE

learning to walk

with Mommy helping me

or sitting in a tree

with Daddy holding me.

☺ **Please tell where you feel safe.**

I FEEL LOVED WITH MY MOMMY AND DADDY!

They have kind eyes that sparkle and lips that turn up into smiles when they see me.

I can see we love one another in our family.

We love Boots too!

☺ **Please tell who has a smile just to see you.**

I AM LEARNING OUR FAMILY VALUES!

They are goals to help us be a good family team!

OUR FAMILY GOALS
- We eat healthy food.
- We use kind words.
- We listen to one another.
- We keep our home tidy.
- I obey Mommy & Daddy.
- We help one another.

☺ **Please tell one of your FAMILY GOALS.**
☺ **I will share ours if you don't have any.**

THE MAGICAL

POWER OF CHOICE

I MAKE GOOD CHOICES BECAUSE:

1. THEY HELP ME BE SAFE;

2. THEY HELP ME BE HAPPY;

3. THEY HELP ME BE HEALTHY;

4. MOMMY AND DADDY WILL BE PROUD OF ME;

5. I WILL BE PROUD OF MYSELF;

6. THEY HELP ME GROW UP STRONG. MAKING GOOD CHOICES IS A MAIN JOB EVEN WHEN WE GROW UP!

I CAN CHOOSE SAFE CLOTHES:

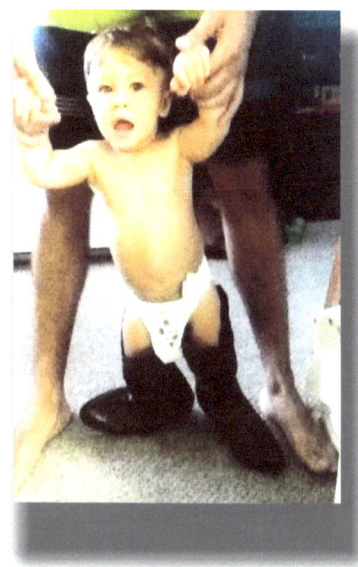

These boots are too big! I might fall!

A fireman's suit is fun, but not on a hot day!

I AM STILL THINKING ABOUT CLOTHES:

I also like my tee shirt, jeans and sneakers.

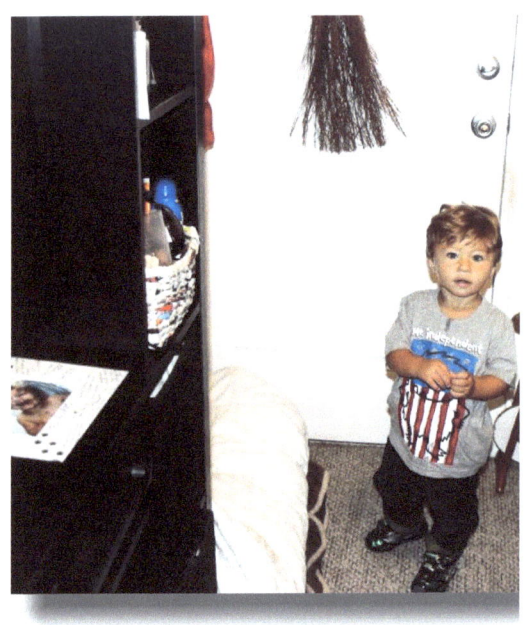

They are safe to run and play in even when it is hot. I choose to wear these clothes!
This is a good choice!

- 😊 **Please tell which clothes you wear when it is cold.**

- 😊 **Please tell which clothes you wear when it is hot.**

I CAN MAKE HAPPY CHOICES:
I can choose a toy to play with.

My puzzle is fun when I have help.

My truck is fun even if I don't have help.
I can ride it. I can play spin the wheels.

Now I must think:

- 😊 Both toys are fun.

- 😊 I need help with the puzzle.

- 😊 I can ride the truck or spin its wheels.

I choose the truck.

I made a good choice!

☺ **Please tell about your favorite toy.**

SOMETIMES CHILDREN MAKE A BAD CHOICE, LIKE

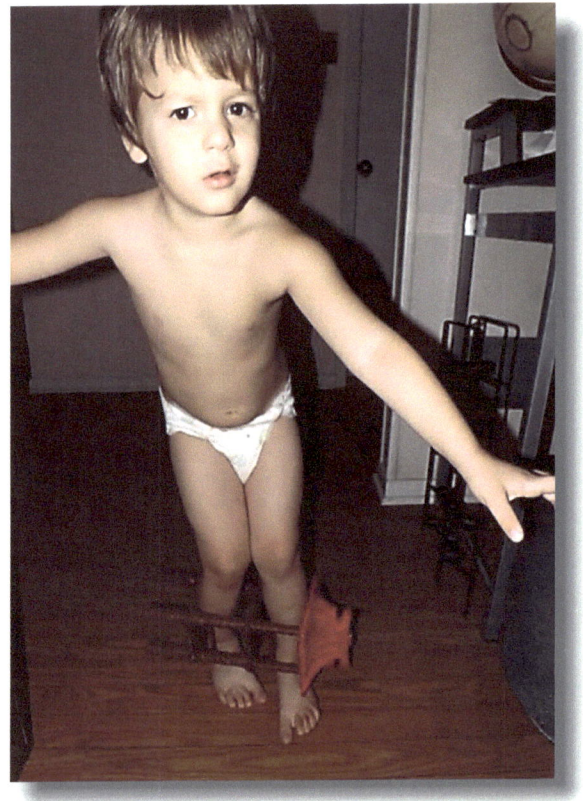

Jaxon putting his feet in a toy!

ONE TIME I MADE A BAD CHOICE, SO
MOMMY HELPED ME THINK ABOUT IT:

She said, "Liam, books are not for tearing up. Books have pictures that are fun to look at and stories for reading. Torn books make messes that you have to clean up. I wonder, Liam, was tearing the book a good choice or a bad choice? I need you to think about it."

THEN I THOUGHT ABOUT IT:

Mommy said, "Books are for looking at pictures and reading, not for tearing."

Her smile left; that was sad.

I had to clean up the mess!

I think that tearing my book was a bad choice!

Next time I'll say, "Hands, books are for reading not tearing!"

😊 Please talk about a bad choice you made.

SOME THINGS ARE NOT A CHOICE:

LEAVING MY ROOM MESSY IS NOT A CHOICE.

Toys hide where I step. They can break or trip me.

BEING FASTENED INTO A SAFE
CAR-SEAT IS NOT A CHOICE.

😃 **Please tell why you need a safe car-seat.**

BEING BORED OR GRUMPY IS NOT A CHOICE.

Alastar may just be tired or lonely. He can choose to do something that makes him happy:

He can choose to breathe in happy air, then blow out grumpy air … five times!

MORE CHOICES:

Take a "my time" break in a favorite place,

and rest on a "froggie" pillow,

or play with "my time toys."

I save these toys for "my time."

EXERCISE MAKES KIDS HAPPY TOO!

Colin exercises on the playground.

☺ **Please tell what your favorite exercise is!**

WHO CAN BE GRUMPY WHEN SINGING A SONG?

☺ **Please won't you sing along with me?!**

THE POWER OF CHOICE SONG
(Melody on www.carolynwatts.net & You Tube)

Oh, deedle deedle dum, deedle deedle dee,
The power of choice belongs to me.
Thinking and choosing what is best for me
Makes it easy to do what is right, you see.
Oh deedle deedle dum dee dee!

Oh, deedle deedle dum, deedle deedle dee,
Silly tongue, candy's not good for me;
It makes my tummy feel sick and my head dizzy;
So I'll think first and eat a fruit or veggie,
Oh deedle deedle dum dee dee!

Oh, deedle deedle dum, deedle deedle dee,
The power of choice belongs to me.
Thinking and choosing what is best for me
Makes my body feel light and my head feel free.
Oh deedle deedle dum dee dee!

Oh deedle deedle dum, deedle deedle dee
It's a wonderful magical thing you see
Deedle deedle dum, deedle deedle doo
The power of choice is for you too!
Deedle deedle dum dee doo!

I hope you and your child enjoyed this book. I encourage you to contact me with your comments and thoughts.

Carolyn Ferrell Watts
cifwatts@gmail.com

Visit my website at www.carolynwatts.net

www.ingramcontent.com/pod-product-compliance
Lightning Source LLC
Chambersburg PA
CBHW041743040426
42444CB00001B/2